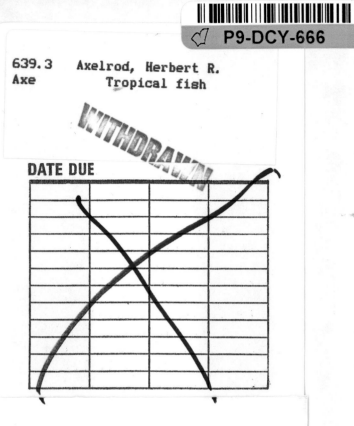

South Sioux City Public Library

2219 Dakota Ave.

South Sioux City, NE 68776

402-494-7545

DEMCO

TROPICAL FISH
KW-020

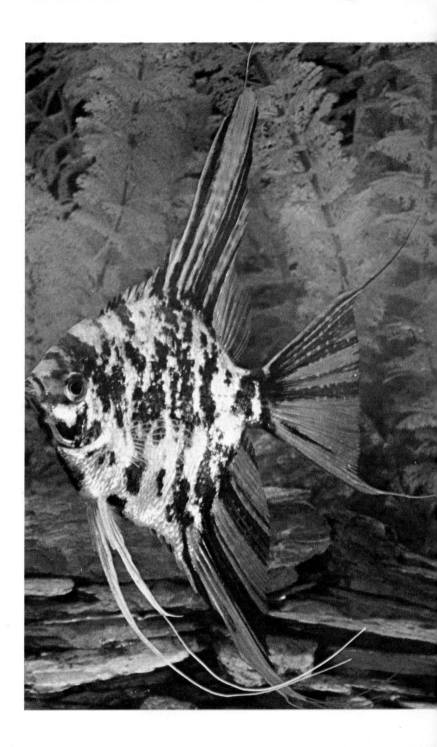

Contents

Photographers: Dr. Herbert R. Axelrod, S. Frank, Michael Gilroy, Dr. Harry Grier, Dr. William T. Innes, B. Kahl, N. Kiselov, Dr. Karl Knaack, Aaron Norman, Klaus Paysan, Penn-Plax Plastics, Hans Joachim Richter, Andre Roth, Southern Tropical Fish Hatchery, R. Stawikowski, Jiri Taborsky, Braz Walker, Wardley Products, K. Zahradka, Rudi Zukal.

Overleaf: A pair of marble angelfish. **Title page:** *A strikingly red Siamese fighting fish.*

t.f.h.

Distributed in the UNITED STATES by T.F.H. Publications, Inc., One T.F.H. Plaza, Neptune City, NJ 07753; in CANADA to the Pet Trade by H & L Pet Supplies Inc., 27 Kingston Crescent, Kitchener, Ontario N2B 2T6; Rolf C. Hagen Ltd., 3225 Sartelon Street, Montreal 382 Quebec; in CANADA to the Book Trade by Macmillan of Canada (A Division of Canada Publishing Corporation), 164 Commander Boulevard, Agincourt, Ontario M1S 3C7; in ENGLAND by T.F.H. Publications Limited, Cliveden House/Priors Way/Bray, Maidenhead, Berkshire SL6 2HP, England; in AUSTRALIA AND THE SOUTH PACIFIC by T.F.H. (Australia) Pty. Ltd., Box 149, Brookvale 2100 N.S.W., Australia; in NEW ZEALAND by Ross Haines & Son, Ltd., 18 Monmouth Street, Grey Lynn, Auckland 2, New Zealand; in SINGAPORE AND MALAYSIA by MPH Distributors (S) Pte., Ltd., 601 Sims Drive, #03/07/21, Singapore 1438; in the PHILIPPINES by Bio-Research, 5 Lippay Street, San Lorenzo Village, Makati Rizal; in SOUTH AFRICA by Multipet Pty. Ltd., 30 Turners Avenue, Durban 4001. Published by T.F.H. Publications, Inc. Manufactured in the United States of America by T.F.H. Publications, Inc.

TROPICAL FISH

DR. HERBERT R. AXELROD

Left: Children enjoy aquariums and will benefit from them greatly, as aquariums are educational as well as fun. Young children, however, should be closely supervised around aquariums, for both their protection and that of the fish. **Below:** When setting up an aquarium, be sure to provide a cover; many fishes, such as the marbled hatchetfish, are capable of jumping out.

Setting Up

Tropical fishes, aquarium fishes...whatever you prefer to call them...can be either all or none of these!

You can have fish you caught in your local pond in the aquarium, or the most exotic Siamese fighting fish kept in an outdoor pond. It doesn't matter. This book will help you get started regardless of what you call them! All fish have the same basic needs for food, shelter and proper environment (water temperature and a degree of neutrality between acid and alkaline pH)...that's what this book is about.

This book has been written with the new hobbyist and his dealer in mind. There are many questions that arise in the mind of the new hobbyist and, as is often the case, his dealer is too busy to answer them all. This book will attempt to answer all the elementary questions in an elementary sort of way. For a more advanced and thorough discussion of the same problems, consult a larger book such as *Exotic Tropical Fishes*.

THE TANK

For some reason or other you

have acquired a certain size aquarium. Let's hope it's not too late to tell you to get the largest size that is practical for your situation, for the larger the aquarium the easier it is to maintain. The size should depend upon your pocketbook, amount of space available, sizes of aquaria available and types of fishes you intend to maintain. The best size for you is an important consideration for your dealer. Give him the measurements of the space in which you intend to place the aquarium.

When you have purchased the aquarium, be sure you have obtained gravel (get at least two pounds for every gallon capacity of the aquarium), a reflector for the top of the aquarium, bulbs for the reflector, a feeding ring, a thermometer, a heater and thermostat if you live in a temperate region, a pump and filter setup if you intend to really do the thing right, some aquarium plants, some fish food and a book on fishes. Note that there was no mention made of fishes! You don't take the fishes home until the aquarium is set up.

Now that you've arrived home with your big bundle of aquarium gadgets, here's what you do:

If your aquarium is small enough to fit into the sink, place it under the faucet and allow it to fill up with warm water of about 95°F (use thermometer). Now turn the spigot away from the tank and

gently pour in the sand or gravel, a little at a time, so that each particle can be washed as it falls into the aquarium. Once all the sand has thus been treated, place the stream of water back onto the aquarium and gently mix the sand about on the bottom, washing it thoroughly until it is perfectly clean. This is easy to tell, for the water coming off the aquarium should be clear. Once this has been achieved, pour out most of the water, using a cup as a scoop (don't try to pour it out by tilting the tank, as you're quite liable to warp the frame and make the tank leak) until most of it is out. Then lift the tank up FROM THE BOTTOM and dry it off. Now place it where it is to remain for quite a while and start looking for a clean piece of white paper or newspaper. Place the paper over the bottom of the aquarium, covering the sand, get a pot or other suitable container and begin filling the aquarium until it is half full of water. When it is half full at 75°F, plant the aquatic vegetation as artistically as possible and fill the balance of the aquarium. If you fill it first and then attempt to plant, you'll find water all over the floor due to the overflow when you put your hands into the tank.

If you have purchased your pump and filter, this is the time to set them up per directions from your dealer. Then put in your heater and thermostat, your thermometer, and then wait. After

A wide variety of aquarium equipment is available at your local pet shop. The owner can help you select the best equipment for your particular needs.

24 hours, if you have an aerator and the temperature is between 72 to 80°F, you may go out and buy the fish. If you have no pump, wait another day or two and then go out and buy the fish, providing your temperature is right. Remember these are tropical fishes and require a temperature of at least 72°F every day of the year. Don't try to place them over a radiator, for they will be boiled when the heat is on and frozen when it is turned off. An aquarium thermostatic heater is just what is necessary; no substitutions, please!

When selecting a place for the aquarium, don't think that "right by the window" is the best place...far from it. Try to select a well-lighted place without getting too much direct sunlight, and try to keep the tank away from chilly exposures, especially if you like to have your windows open in the winter time.

Above: This tank has been aquascaped with artificial plants, cured driftwood, shale, a plastic ornament, and a natural background. Furnishings such as these are available at your local pet shop. *Right:* This tank is an all-glass set-up which is outfitted with living plants. The silver-tip tetras are about to spawn among the fine thickets of the plants.

Selecting Plants

It is possible to state our aim in setting up our tropical home aquarium: "Try to imitate the natural surroundings of the fish we are to keep as pets." Most fish come from ponds or rivers where there is a certain amount of natural vegetation and a soil bottom. It is best suited for our purposes to use sand rather than soil for the sake of appearance. Sand is not only cleaner, but it represents a better rooting medium for plants.

Different plants grow well in different types of aquarium

settings. The depth to which they are planted as well as the amount of light they are to receive are very important to consider before they are purchased. Let's take a look at various plants that are available for the home aquarium.

Cabomba caroliniana, commonly called simply cabomba, is a very lovely plant. It looks good in bunches of five or six strands. The fan-shaped appearance of the leaves may suggest the popular name "fanwort." This plant needs plenty of light and gets terribly stringy when light is not available. If the tank is placed near a window where north light is always available during the daylight hours, the plants will do very well.

When planting, it is wise to snip off the bottom inch or so of the plants and place them about an inch into the sand so they may take root and not float up.

Anacharis or more scientifically *Elodea canadensis* is another plant that is very commonly found in home aquaria. It, too, does well in a lighted aquarium and should be planted in bunches.

Since anacharis and cabomba grow to very long lengths under the proper conditions, it is wise to plant them toward the rear of the aquarium so they will not grow in front of smaller plants and thus shield them from enjoying eyes.

Milfoil or *Myriophyllum spicatum* is a plant closely resembling fanwort, but it is much more delicate because of its lacy leaves. It, like all plants, will grow toward light, so it is best to plant it in the back or sides of the aquarium where the most light is allowed to enter. It is a fast-growing plant and is widely used in spawning egg layers.

Vallisneria americana and *Sagittaria gigantea* are two types of popular tape grasses. They are attractive narrow-leafed type plants that grow rather slowly as compared with the other plants mentioned. They produce young plants by sending out runners. These plants should not be placed deeply into the sand. Never cover the crown of the plant with sand. Rather, let it stick above the sand's surface.

The *Cryptocoryne* plants are those plants that are more broad-leafed and need much less light to keep them going than do any of the other types. They too should be planted with the crown above sand level. As the leaves fade and die, it is wise to snip them off at the bottom rather than let them dirty the tank by accumulating and decomposing. Dwarf and larger species of this plant are available and are rather expensive when compared with anacharis, cabomba and myriophyllum.

Echinodorus bleheri, or more commonly the Amazon sword plant, is an ideal centerpiece for a tank deep enough to maintain it. It is senseless to place an Amazon sword plant into a tank lower than 12 inches deep. The plant will

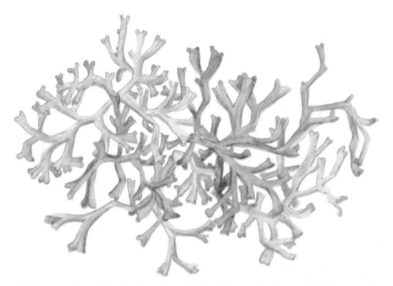

Artist's rendering of the floating plant Riccia fluitans. *Plants such as this are often used for spawning purposes.*

grow to two or three feet in length, depending upon the depth of the water. It should be planted with the crown above the sand line and sometimes needs to be weighted with a piece of lead until it roots. It is truly the prince of aquarium plants, and a good reproducer will make an attractive setting with its daughter plants all around it. When the runner starts growing out, it is wise to weight the runner onto the sand with a small rock or piece of lead. The daughter plants may be severed from the parent plant as soon as they root.

Never use humus or soil of any kind to "fertilize" your aquarium sand. The fishes will take care of that job. Should the plants begin to lose their green color and become stringy, it simply implies that they are not getting enough light, and more light should be offered to them. This is accomplished with a reflector made to fit neatly on the top of the aquarium. Some reflectors have fluorescent lights rather than ordinary incandescent lights. These are usually as efficient as sunlight and a lot cheaper to operate than the usual type of bulb, and they give off less heat.

Some floating plants like *Lemna minor* and *Spirodela polyrhiza,* the familiar duckweeds, are usually only a nuisance and should be avoided. Sometimes they, as well as riccia, salvinia, lesser bladderwort and water hyacinth, are used for spawning purposes.

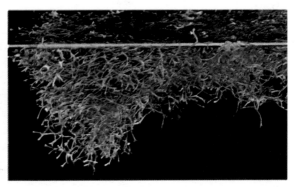

This assemblage of aquarium plants includes Riccia *(above);* Cabomba *(left);* Vallisneria gigantea *(below, left);* Elodea *(below, right);* Cryptocoryne *(opposite, top left);* Ludwigia *(opposite, top right); and* Vallisneria americana *(opposite, bottom).*

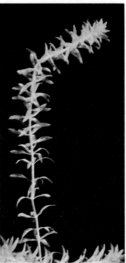

The Gravel

A word or two about the sand and setting it into the tank. The sand usually comes directly to your fish dealer from the manufacturer. It is not true sand, but rather a fine gravel. It contains much dirt which, though not deadly to the fish, is unsightly. The sand should be thoroughly cleaned in small batches at a time by placing it in a bucket and running water through it constantly, if the tank is too large to be handled as described earlier. This should be done until the water runs off clear. The sand should be stirred constantly while it is being washed.

After the aquarium has been thoroughly washed and set in its final appointed place, then and only then should the sand be placed into it. Fill it from the back to the front, sloping the sand preferably in a horseshoe shape. After the sand is in place, a sheet of white paper should be laid over it and the water slowly poured onto the paper so as not to disturb your arrangement of the sand. NEVER FILL THE TANK WITH

Below: A pre-potted Echinodorous bleheri *plant. Pre-potted plants are available at your local pet shop; they contain nutrients which allow the plants to be placed right in the aquarium without having to wait until the gravel medium is ready.* **Opposite:** *A lovely zebra mbuna,* Pseudotropheus zebra.

Opposite: *When arranging gravel in the tank, the bed should vary according to the height of the aquarium, and it should be arranged so that the gravel slopes down from the rear of the aquarium.* **Above:** *Many decorative items for your gravel bed are available at your local pet shop.* **Below:** *A fun pastime for tropical fish hobbyists is collecting stamps with aquarium fishes as a theme. Many countries issue such stamps.*

Above: A good gravel medium is important for a healthy aquarium environment. Be sure your gravel is rounded and not sharp, as many fishes will mouth it or move it around during their daily travels. *Opposite:* A long-finned rosy barb, Puntius conchonius.

SAND AND WATER BEFORE IT IS FINALLY LOCATED. The strain may burst the sides or bottom. It is wise to allow the water to "age" for a few days prior to placing the fishes and plants into the tank. Sometimes water contains a chlorine concentration strong enough to kill both fishes and plants. Anti-chlorine tablets or drops are available to remove this chlorine and condition the water.

Make sure that the water is of the proper temperature before the fishes are introduced, and exercise care in putting the fishes into the water. Pour them very gently, having the container in the water all the time, and just tilt the container so the fish can swim out. Be sure to always have the cover on, as most fish are good jumpers, especially when they are confined.

Above: Your selection of fishes depends upon many factors: the cost of the fishes, the size of your aquarium, and the types of fishes available in your area. Cardinal tetras, Paracheirodon axelrodi *(named in honor of the author),* are usually readily available. *Right:* Red swordtails are popular aquarium fishes.

Selecting Fishes

Your selection of fishes depends almost entirely upon the sort of stock at your dealer. It would be difficult for this book to mention all the possible combinations of fishes that get along well together, so only a handful of fishes will be discussed, more or less a representative sample of the many kinds of fishes that can be maintained in a home aquarium.

For purposes of discussion in this book, tropical fishes are broken up into four different categories: egg layers, livebearers, bubblenest builders and scavengers. The *egg layers* are those kinds of fish that lay eggs in order to reproduce. The *livebearers* are those fishes that

have live young born to them. The *bubblenest builders* are those fish that build a nest of bubbles to support their fry at the surface of the water. They are like egg layers, of course, since they do lay eggs, but their use of a bubblenest in their reproductive behavior makes them sufficiently different from other egg layers to merit their being treated separately. All bubblenest builders are also air-breathing (using atmospheric air), though not all air-breathers are bubblenest builders. Finally, there are the *scavengers*, which are the fishes that feed off the bottom; their scavenging habits have nothing to do with their breeding habits.

Below: A cardinal tetra. Opposite: A mature oscar, Astronotus ocellatus, *photographed as it flares its branchiostegal membranes to show its displeasure about something.*

Above: A female guppy giving birth to a live baby. Guppies are easy to breed and are usually the first fish recommended for the beginning aquarist. *Right:* These male guppies were raised in Moscow and were the result of intensive inbreeding.

Livebearers

THE GUPPY

Heading the list of suitable livebearers comes the very popular guppy. Scientifically, the guppy is known as *Poecilia reticulata*. It is without a doubt the hardiest, most easily bred and most tolerant of all the known livebearing tropical fishes. Add to this a varied, intense coloration, perfect behavior and a diet that includes everything known to fish dieticians and you have an excellent fish for beginners.

The male guppy is the individual of the species. To him nature has given the color and variety of pattern that would make a peacock jealous. The females are more stereotyped and all look alike. Females, too, are a bit larger than the males, but neither gets much larger than 1½ inches in length.

Being livebearers, the males have a modified anal fin with which they are able to impregnate the female. This is an early sexual characteristic which makes identification of males easy, even before their color becomes apparent.

The usual brood of a female guppy may range from 30 to 75 youngsters, but records count as high as 125. A normal female will have a brood every month, so you can see that it doesn't take too long before you have a stock of guppies!

As far as temperature goes, guppies can do well in a range of from 70 to 90°F, though the ideal is about 75°F. If possible, their aquarium should be heavily planted with bushy plants (like *Cabomba* or *Elodea*) so the new-born fry can hide from their cannibalistic parents. Once the fry have had a few days of growth "under their belt," the parents are no longer able to eat them and the family gets along just fine.

Guppies originated in Trinidad, but they have been so adaptable to conditions that they are found all over the world, having been introduced into various situations by ardent aquarists.

Many varieties of guppies are available with colors of the rainbow being displayed on larger and longer fins. The price of the guppy is usually very moderate, though for some of the fancier strains you might be asked to pay a relatively high price! Look at it this way: if you're going to raise fish you might as well raise specimens you're going to be proud of, so invest a bit more in better breeding stock and really have something when you're finished. Your dealer will surely purchase your excess stock if it's worthwhile. Thus you can make your hobby pay as it goes just from this little fish alone.

For the beginning aquarist, the livebearers are the most interesting and fascinating fish to breed. With no particular trouble they may multiply easily and rapidly, producing a new group every month or so.

Most livebearers have one distinct habit that makes them seem rather ferocious compared to the rest of the animal world; that is, they are inclined to eat their own young. With but few exceptions, the livebearers must be watched so that the youngsters can be taken away from the parents as soon as they are dropped from the mother fish.

There is a device that is very helpful in that it separates the young from the mother fish, and that is a breeding trap. When the fry are dropped from the mother fish, they fall right through the slatted bottom of the breeding trap and either swim away into the rest of the tank or are protected by a combination of the breeding and nursery trap.

There is usually no difficulty in getting guppies and other viviparous (Latin for "livebearing") fishes to mate. All that seems necessary is to have a member of each sex in the same tank and they will start to raise a family. The sexes are easily distinguishable in this type of fish, as the female has a fully developed anal fin while the male has a long, pointed gonopodium, and it is with this gonopodium that he is able to fertilize the female. Most of the viviparous young mature and are able to reproduce at three months after birth.

If we attempt to set down a general rule for breeding livebearers, we would be making generalizations that would be very limited and not helpful at all to the beginning aquarist. We will discuss some of the general considerations that we must make for raising these livebearers, but keep in mind that they are only general, and a more thorough understanding of each fish can be

The usual size of a brood of guppies ranges from 30 to 75 young; however, deliveries of well over 100 are not uncommon.

Above: Guppies have been bred by tropical fish hobbyists for many years. The first fancy guppies were merely colorful fish without any clear patterns or any similarity between related strains. They came from the earliest of the common guppies. **Opposite, top left:** A very plain male guppy. Later on, fancier strains were developed, such as the half-black guppies and the albino form of the half-blacks shown at upper right side. Most of these varieties were developed in Singapore. **Opposite, bottom:** Additional forms, sometimes called "snakeskins," began to appear. Today, guppies are available in many different colors and with different types of finnage.

had by reading further on each species of fish.

It is best to choose the fish you want to raise according to their physical characteristics. Size, color and vigor are important physical factors to be taken into consideration.

Choose only those fish with the best color, as this physical characteristic is transmitted from the parent fish to the brood much in the same way that our physical characteristics are transmitted from parent to offspring. If you are going to take the trouble to raise fishes, you might just as well raise good fishes with color and stature that you will admire and that will be admired by your friends. There is a certain feeling that one gets when he has raised his own fish, a feeling of satisfaction and a feeling of success. The fish he raised may be the most terrible looking specimens of the family, but to the aquarist-father or aquarist-mother, they are the most beautiful. So raise fish that you will be more than pleased to display. Do not waste your time and effort with poorly colored fish.

When female guppies show signs of being "loaded" (a dark area in the anal region), they should be separated from the rest of the fishes if possible. Care should be exercised in the handling of these fish. This separation has a dual purpose. First, it prevents the mother fish from being molested by other fishes that are around the tank; and secondly, if she should drop her young before she is transferred to another tank, they will surely be eaten by the other fish. This tank, the delivery tank, need not be larger than one gallon, for as soon as the mother fish drops her young she should be removed or she will make a good meal of them. The mother fish should be kept well fed while she is in this tank, waiting to drop, so she will not have too great a desire to chase her little youngsters around for a quick meal. It is a good idea to have this tank very heavily planted. Having dense anacharis and vallisneria in the tank and allowing some cabomba to float around the surface will greatly aid the young fish in hiding from its parent. Remember to take all precautions when shifting the mother fish from one tank to the next. If possible, take the gallon of water from her original tank; if not, make sure that the water has the same temperature, hardness and pH as that of the original aquarium. The temperature should be checked with a thermometer and should not be more than 2°F above or below the temperature of the original tank. The hardness may be checked with a water hardness testing kit and the pH with a pH test kit.

After the baby fish are born, the mother should be removed immediately and placed back in

Choose only those guppies with the best color and health for breeding. Good offspring cannot come from mediocre parents.

her own tank. It is a good idea to have more than one female in the tank into which you intend to place the mother fish. Usually after giving birth females are weak, and when the male fish chase them, they seem very annoyed.

A very complete study has been made of the sex life of the guppy by prominent aquarists. They found that a male fish would try to get to a female fish even if she were placed in a jar separated from the rest of the fish in the tank. Should an anesthetized female be allowed to drop to the bottom, the male guppies will continually try to stick her with their gonopodiums. A freshly killed female in a similar position would either be eaten or totally disregarded. Actual contact between male and female is necessary for fertilization. There are few male animals that persist so strenuously in chasing a pregnant female as the male guppy.

If there are no other female fishes in the community tank, then it would be better to leave the mother fish in a tank by herself for a few days so she can recuperate. The baby fish should be left by themselves in their own tank for as long a period as possible, preferably until they are mature. After they are three or four weeks old they should be transferred to a tank with rooted plants in it. If they

*Opposite: Bill Hearin's hifin platy variatus. **Right:** Beautifully colored sunset platy variatus. **Below:** The same strain as the sunset platies above, these fish were developed 20 years earlier, before the strain was perfected.*

When selecting guppies for your tank, avoid listless fish, especially those with tattered fins and missing scales.

are put into the community aquarium too early, they are liable to be eaten by the other fish or else they will have a tough job competing with the larger fishes for food.

Even though the young of livebearing species are born alive, they nevertheless were once little eggs in one of the egg sacs in their mother's body. The body of the female livebearer has several sacs which, we can say for our purposes, hold the eggs. When the male fertilizes the female by sticking her in the anal region with his gonopodium, the eggs start to grow in one sac at a time. This means that a female need be fertilized only once to have several broods of young fish. Thus we have a reason for the apparent "virgin births" reported by many hobbyists.

As the eggs mature into young fish, there is a characteristic black spot near the anus (vent) of the mother fish. This spot is more pronounced in the lighter species and is caused by the presence of young, unborn fish, and as the time for birth draws near, it gets blacker and blacker.

Baby fishes should be fed fine, powdered food. This food is prepared commercially and is very reasonable. Infusoria should also be available to young fish. As the fish get older, they can eat coarser foods. Sifted daphnia and newly hatched brine shrimp are also excellent foods for newborn fishes. Daphnia are small aquatic crustaceans of various genera, the most common of which is the genus *Daphnia*; regardless of their taxonomic status, they are usually sold under the name "daphnia."

If you are having difficulty breeding livebearers, there are several sources of trouble that should be checked. If you have bred the same fish too often, she may stop breeding for a while. Sometimes the fish are undernourished. Your best bet here is to feed them some live food and several varieties of dried

Healthy guppies may live longer than three years if they are given good food and are maintained properly.

A group of platies and swordtails with elongated dorsal fins.

food. A good idea is to chop a small piece of fresh meat into fine particles and feed it to your fish one piece at a time. If you just dump it all right into the tank, some may get hidden in the crevices and start to decay. Another cause of breeding interference could be stale water or water with an improper hardness or pH. Checks should be made on the hardness and pH as well as the temperature. If all of these causes are eliminated and the fish still fail to breed, then they are in all probability too young to breed and may still have a few weeks to mature, or they are too old. Old fish may be recognized by having a hump in their back. Compare them to young fish and this physical characteristic is easily recognized. The average livebearer matures at about eight months and may live for three to five years.

MOLLIES

The familiar contraction of the old generic name *Mollienisia* to the common name molly is evidence of the popularity of the several species of this genus.

Mollies are found in nature all along the coastal waters of the eastern Americas from South Carolina to Venezuela. They have been found both far out in the ocean and inland in fresh water, but there is little doubt that they favor a brackish water (part fresh water, part sea water)

environment. For this reason salt must be added to the aquarium in which these beauties are maintained.

The reasons for the popularity of mollies are many: first and foremost, they are inexpensive. Secondly, they are fairly hardy and do well in unheated aquaria. Third, they are colorful, always active and peaceful members of the community aquarium.

Scientifically, we recognize four species of mollies, but the hobbyist can more easily recognize two groups. The *sailfin mollies* are so named for the large dorsal fin which the male sports. This large dorsal fin may have from 12 to 19 rays in it. Even though the females show only a small dorsal fin, it is very easily proven that she has just as many rays as the male. The two species commonly called sailfins are *Poecilia latipinna*, found from Mexico north to South Carolina, and *Poecilia velifera*, found in the shore waters of Yucatan.

Mollies having a shorter dorsal fin and a dorsal ray count of from eight to 11 are known to us as *Poecilia sphenops* and *Poecilia latipunctala*. The latter is found only in the Rio Tamesi and its tributaries in Mexico, but the sphenops may be found from Mexico to Venezuela and points in between.

Poecilia latipinna is the green sailfin molly. The olive dorsal edge leads to a beautifully silvered

A pair of silver sailfin mollies, Poecilia velifera. *Note the interesting patterns on their tail fins.*

lateral surface adorned with from six to eight rows of black dots. The belly is more whitish than silver. The male sports an extremely large dorsal fin which may run as long as three-quarters of the entire body length and up to 1½ inches in height. The female has a smaller dorsal. In length, the female may be slightly larger than the male, but specimens of up to four inches in length are quite commonly found in the bays about southern Florida. Some black varieties are found in nature. Black varieties of *P. sphenops* and *P. velifera* were also developed. When the black variety of *P. velifera* is crossed with the black variety of *P. latipinna*, a strain known as the permablack molly is developed. These crosses have an all-black brood. Inbreeding of black mollies will usually result in

Above: Red wagtail platies, Xiphophorus maculatus, *like all other platies, are closely related to the swordtails.* **Opposite, top left:** Xiphophorus variatus *is the only* Xiphophorus *species in which males and females are colored differently.* **Opposite, top right:** *Hifin swordtails.* **Opposite, below:** *Many fancy platies and swordtails were developed by Dr. Myron Gordon (late teacher of the author) in his New York laboratories. These six photos were taken in 1940. Left column, top to bottom—blue moon platy, salt-and-pepper platy, gold platy. Right column, top to bottom—red platy, green tuxedo platy, red tuxedo platy.*

a gradual reappearance of the natural green coloration.

The orange dorsal sailfin molly is the black variety of *P. latipinna* in which a beautiful orange edge has been added to the dorsal fin. A newer strain of the orange dorsal molly is now appearing with the same orange band on the outer margin of the caudal fin. The silvery green molly with the orange margin on the tail fin is not *P. latipinna*, but a variety of *P. sphenops*. The golden molly, a pinkish yellow variety with black eyes, is a result of crossing the albino variety of *P. latipinna* with the normal strain. Albino forms are common.

Poecilia sphenops is found in salt water, brackish water and fresh water. There appears to be no significant difference in the specimens taken from the different environments other than size. The more salty the water, the larger the fish grows. All kinds of color variations are found in this fish. The wild variety is light gray-green with a bluish or aqua cast. There are small dark spots unevenly spread all over the sides, and the belly may run from gray-white to silver-blue. Males may show a faint series of vertical bars on their sides and extremes of color in the caudal fin. Females are more uniformly colored and are usually plain, getting to be an inch or more longer than the three-inch male. Black, short-finned mollies are usually of this species, as is the popular liberty molly. This liberty molly, once an aquarium favorite, is no longer being produced in great quantities. It is recognized by the brilliant colors in the dorsal and caudal fins of the otherwise silvery male.

In all small-dorsalled mollies, maturity and full development may take six to eight months, while in the sailfinned mollies we can wait a full year for the large dorsal to fully develop.

Food for the molly is an important consideration. While most fishes are carnivorous, the molly is herbivorous. That is, in everyday language, the molly is a vegetarian. True enough, mollies will greedily take worms, daphnia and other live foods, but they will not subsist for very long on this diet. Chopped lettuce, spinach and aquatic plants are a necessity for this fish. The location of the aquarium in a very sunny position where algae will grow rapidly in copious amounts is a prime requisite in maintaining these fishes successfully. It seems that when conditions are right, the molly will be perpetually picking at the glass, leaves and whatever else will act as a holdfast for the algae. The familiar "shimmies," so common to mollies, is caused by improper diet. A special molly food is on the market which contains a great deal of finely chopped, dried vegetable matter. A food of this sort is a must for all vegetarian fishes.

Sailfin mollies come in many varieties. These fish, Poecilia latipinna, *sport the typical sailfin.*

Mollies are best bred out of doors in large pools or ponds. They suffer little in temperatures between 65 and 90°F, providing there is plenty of room. A large pair of mollies requires a ten-gallon aquarium all to themselves, with as much vegetation growing as possible.

Breeding is more or less automatic. Parents will not eat their young unless they are hungry. Fry must have small plant life (algae) to eat. "Green" water is the best place in which to raise these young fish.

Sex is easily determined, as the male has the modified anal fin with which he must make contact with the female in order to fertilize her. Great care should be exercised in handling "heavy" females, and they should not be moved when in this full condition.

Above: A female swordtail releasing a newborn. As the baby is born, the mother fish curves her body in a mild jerk to send it on its way. At this point, the young fish still carries a little reserve food in its yolk sac. **Opposite, top:** Two sailfin molly males dancing before a female. The dorsal fin of the female is generally smaller than that of the male. **Opposite, bottom:** A recently developed variety, a stubby-bodied sailfin black molly with a lyretail. This fish was produced in Singapore.

Though prone to fungus when kept in water without sufficient salt, they can be easily cured by the addition of non-iodized salt (two tablespoons per gallon) and two drops of a 5% solution of methylene blue per gallon of water. It is the author's practice to have this dye in the water with mollies at all times.

In addition, mollies are easily kept in the marine aquarium.

SWORDTAILS

The swordtail is scientifically known as *Xiphophorus helleri*. It originated in Mexico and adjacent areas, and wild specimens are usually a dull green. But largely through the efforts of fish geneticists this fish has been produced in a great variety of colors and color patterns. Bright reds, blood reds, greens, blacks, golds and albino varieties are an everyday sight in the fish store. Some varieties even have a black lace-like tail and fin color, known as wagtail, added to these beautiful colors; thus we find red wagtail swordtails, gold wagtail swordtails, etc.

The swordtail is another easygoing livebearer that has fairly large broods every 28 days or so. The males are distinguished by the sword-like extension on the tail fin. Both males and females are colored alike, however, and they attain the same approximate size, sometimes up to three inches. They eat all kinds of dried and live foods and are extremely interesting aquarium fishes.

They do well at 75°F and welcome a pinch of non-iodized salt added to their aquarium water. As a general rule, add one teaspoonful of salt to every two gallons of water. The coarse salt is best. As with most livebearers, they are unhappy in freshly drawn water, and their water should be aged as long as possible.

PLATIES

The platies are known scientifically as *Xiphophorus maculatus and X. variatus*. Both species are excellent aquarium fishes. They both come in many different color varieties and finnage varieties. Both species are less aggressive than the swordtail, and both are smaller as well; of the three species *X. maculatus* is the smallest.

Since it is possible to cross all the platies with all the swordtails, we would expect to find exactly the same color varieties among the platies as we do among the swordtails. This is the case, and we find wagtail platies in all colors, as we do ordinary platies in many different color varieties.

Platies need exactly the same care as the swordtails and their gestation period is just about the same.

Xiphophorus variatus. *Both platy species come in a variety of colors and with different finnage.*

Above: An ornate tetra, Hyphessobrycon ornatus. ***Right:*** *A pair of long-finned rosy barbs,* Puntius conchonius.

Egg Layers

The oviparous or egg-laying fishes are quite different physically than livebearing fishes. Many have no apparent sexual differences, and this makes sexing quite a difficult, though not impossible, job. Each species usually has some sexual difference to be observed, but there is no single general rule to follow for sexing all egg layers.

The breeding of egg layers requires recognition of the sexes and a separation of the fishes into distinct sexes so the fish may be brought into breeding condition apart from members of the opposite sex. For each species represented in this book, we will try to describe the sex differences where they are apparent.

Generally speaking, the males have more brilliant colors while the females are heavier in body. Most males, too, have longer anal or dorsal fins.

BLACK TETRA

The black tetra, *Gymnocorymbus ternetzi*, is a rather active and semi-aggressive fish. Though not recommended for community tanks containing smaller fishes, they are very nice for the larger fish community tank.

Successful breeding of the black tetra is more a matter of successfully conditioning the breeders than a matter of technique. The heavy-bodied females should be separated from the males and allowed a week in an aquarium all to themselves. They should be allowed to gorge themselves on live foods. They show a partiality for freshly caught flies (which should be killed first), and they make a mad swipe at them when they are dropped onto the surface of the water. When a week of heavy feeding and conditioning has been afforded them, the females should be placed into a freshly set up aquarium at least of the ten-gallon size (the larger the better). The entire center portion of the tank should be heavily planted with dense bunch plants or artificial spawning grasses, of which Spanish moss is the best. The males should be placed in with the females (in a ratio of one to one) after the females have been in the spawning tank for at least 24 hours.

The tank should not contain any snails, as they will eat the eggs. Spawning takes place by the male and female dashing into the clumps of plants and scattering many eggs. If they don't eat the eggs as they lay them, then they will surely devour the youngsters as soon as they hatch out. The eggs are semi-adhesive and are rather easily seen under a good light. All the fish should be removed after spawning and the young raised in the spawning tank. Infusoria should be cultured as soon as the spawning is completed. Chopped lettuce should be added to the culture. When the young hatch out, they should be left in an aquarium that will get plenty of light all day and artificial light all night. This constant light should be offered them until they are large enough to take freshly hatched brine shrimp and sifted daphnia. Most youngsters starve to death in the early stages of development.

OTHER TETRAS

Besides the black tetra there are many other species sold under the name "tetra," and many of them are both more peaceful and more colorful than *Gymnocorymbus*. The cardinal and neon tetras (*Paracheirodon axelrodi* and *Paracheirodon innesi* respectively) are small, colorful, peaceful fishes that are usually available and always popular because of their bright colors. They are not among the most interesting of aquarium fishes, but they are highly decorative and easy to care for, although not easy to breed and raise. Other popular tetras include the lemon tetra (*Hyphessobrycon pulchripinnis*), the serpae tetra (*Hyphessobrycon serpae* and related species), the flame tetra (*Hyphessobrycon flammeus*), and many others, including a true oddity, the blind cave fish (*Astyanax fasciatus mexicanus*, formerly called *Anoptichthys jordani*), an eyeless fish that nevertheless finds its way

around the aquarium very well. Closely allied to the tetras are the pencilfishes, very peaceful and attractive species that are often available and usually very inexpensive; most of the small pencilfishes are in the genus *Nannostomus*.

ANGELFISH

In the German publication *Wochenschrift fur Aquarien und Terrarien Kunde* of July 1932, there appeared an article on the home of the angelfish written by a Mr. Praetorius. This gentleman is well known for his accurate information on this species, and we are herewith presenting the

A long-finned neon tetra, Paracheirodon innesi. *Neon tetras are easy to care for, although they are not easy fish to breed.*

Above, left: Corkscrew vallisneria. *Above, top right:* A black neon tetra, Hyphessobrycon herbertaxelrodi *(narned in honor of the author).* *Above, lower left:* A flame tetra, Hyphessobrycon flammeus. *Above, lower right:* A lemon tetra, Hyphessobrycon pulchripinnis. *Opposite:* A small group of long-finned black tetras.

"meat" from his writing. The translation is freely taken.

Even though there has been much written about this fish, there hasn't been too much reported on his home life. I am, therefore, trying to portray him as I see him here (Mr. Praetorius lives in Santarem, State of Para in Brazil) in his home waters. First, concerning his range: where it begins I do not know (angelfish have been observed and recovered from waters as far north as the Demerara River near Georgetown, Guyana). However, in numerous travels to Breves, Camata, Gurupa, Almirin, and other spots, I have not been able to find him. This is not to mean that he doesn't occur there, but the real region is not more than 150 to 200 miles upstream. At this point (Santarem), where the Tapajoz River flows into the Amazon, his occurrence is such that he is no longer a king, but only an ordinary fish.

In the Tapajoz River he is found only on the left bank, in what is called the *varje*. Along the right varje is more or less a tideland, where the land is partly or wholly submerged when high water is in. There are no angelfish to be found in midstream either, for only close to the banks, where plants are heavy, do we see the king angelfish. The very best time to see this fellow is during the dry season when the rivers are low. The banks are then lined with the flooded cane growth, the so-called *canarana* and *premenbeke*. The stalks of the first are covered with small, stiff hairs which prick the skin when touched. Below the water level these fine hairs become long, fine roots, very much like the water hyacinth. At the edge and under these plants are great numbers of fish, among them *Pterophyllum scalare*. Proceeding slowly in a canoe along the edge of these growths, you can observe groups of from 15 to 20 specimens. They stay very close to the vegetation, ready to disappear at the slightest sound.

Normally, *Pterophyllum scalare* is accompanied by another cichlid, *Cichlasoma festivum*, which is even more numerous. To describe the actions of the angelfish in this environment would make him sound anything but kingly, for the fish is extremely timid and humble. So easily terrified is he that if one makes a sudden motion with the rudder or the arm, he shoots out of the water, falls flat on the surface and just lies there, making only feeble and senseless efforts. One can easily catch him by hand when he's in this condition. This is very amusing to the natives, who have only contempt for the species, and, consequently, they call him "Pacu Doido," which means "crazy surface fish." They also call him "Acara Bandeira," which means "flag acara."

Around January, when the

A pair of angelfish, Pterophyllum scalare. *Angelfish are among the most popular cichlids, and they are available in a number of shades and finnage varieties.*

rivers start to rise, the angelfish starts to spawn. Great areas along the banks are flooded and the plant growth is heavy. Matted vegetation forms a carpet under which one finds all kind of fishes. This is not too good for the baby angels, as their parents are in the midst of all their enemies, and they seem easily driven away from their spawn. I have seen many small swarms of baby angelfish, with their parents nowhere to be seen.

As is the case with all fishes, the angel is very difficult to trap during the high water period. There is, however, an unsporting way of seeing if the angelfish is about. One strikes the water a sharp blow with the flat side of the paddle or a broad stick. Instantly all the angels in the area break the water and jump rather high into the air.

As strange as it seems, beautiful specimens as we know of them in the aquarium are rarely found in the rivers. Due to their numerous encounters with their enemies, their fins are always in a ragged condition.

In order to breed the angel, there is a question that must be answered first: Are you interested in commercial spawning procedures, or is it just that a pair of angelfish have spawned in your community aquarium and you want to be able to bring the young

Opposite, top: A pencilfish, Nannostomus beckfordi. *Opposite, center:* Bleeding heart tetras, Hyphessobrycon rubrostigma. *Opposite, bottom:* older angelfish, Pterophyllum scalare. *Right:* A pair of black phantom tetras, Megalamphodus megalopterus.

through? Whichever category you are in, the following information will be of value.

Procuring breeding stock is of prime importance when dealing with the angelfish. There are several ways one can obtain stock: buy breeding pairs which are guaranteed to be mated pairs; buy a spawn of small fish and bring them up to breeding size in a very large aquarium, hoping that a few will mate and thus pair off; or purchase a dozen medium size angelfish and bring them to maturity in the same aquarium, hoping that these fish will pair up.

To purchase a mated pair is prohibitively expensive. Not only is there the initial outlay of cash, but there is the gamble that the pair will not continue spawning under new conditions. Sometimes the change of water might not suit them, one of the pair might die an early death, or the pair might be "spawned out." This is the least desirable way to obtain breeding stock, but if time is of the essence, there is no other way.

The most desirable manner of obtaining breeding stock is the group pairing method. Purchase as large a group of smaller-than-breeding-size fish as you can safely raise to maturity in the tank space available. As the fish reach breeding size, you will note that certain pairs will tend to alienate themselves from the rest of the group. They will seem to be fighting almost constantly between

the two of them, but should another fish try to attack either one, the other will come to its rescue. There is good reason to believe that this pair of fish will mate, so remove them to a ten to 15-gallon aquarium heavily planted with Amazon sword plants or giant sagittaria. If you prefer to breed the fish commercially, then place a slate (tilted onto the side of the glass) in with them. The pair should spawn within a few weeks if they are brought to breeding condition by constant feedings of daphnia, tubifex and small fishes. As other pairs manifest themselves, they should also be separated.

If perchance the fish are brought to maturity in a very large aquarium and there is no risk of overcrowding as the fish get larger, then it may be possible to leave the entire batch of sexually matured fish together and merely remove the eggs from the aquarium as the fish spawn. This is not too desirable a method of commercially propagating the angelfish, as many spawns may be lost due to the cannibalism of the other fish. It is the most accepted practice to separate mated pairs and keep them in their own breeding tank.

Once a pair has spawned, there are two possibilities: either allow the parents to tend the fry until they are freeswimming, or remove the eggs (or the parents) and raise the fry without their parents. There are several functions that parent angelfish must fulfill, and if you intend to remove the parents then there must be artificial means for fulfilling these functions. One of the functions is to keep the eggs clean of bacteria and sediment. The parent fish help keep the eggs clean by a process known as "fanning the spawn." This is accomplished by one of the breeders maintaining a position directly over the spawn, and by a constant movement of its fins it is able to maintain an unceasing flow of water over the developing eggs. This not only keeps the eggs clear of bacteria (by keeping natural sediment from being deposited on the spawn), but also assures the

spawn of a supply of freshly oxygenated water. Developing eggs need oxygen as much as the free-swimming fry do. The usual manner in which these parental functions are taken care of without the breeders is to place the eggs (which have been deposited, assumedly, either on the slate or on the leaf of a relatively stiff-leafed plant) in such a position that a fine stream of air from a good air stone is directed right over the top of them. This is easily accomplished by tilting the slate, eggs down, against the side of the hatching aquarium and placing the air releaser underneath it. Too much of an air current will be detrimental to the fry as they start

A pair of angelfish. Wild angelfish are reported to be rather timid.

to hatch out. They remain attached to the slate by a rather delicate thread of sticky material which seems to come from the head, and the strong current of air might tear them loose and injure them. Some fry, however, always seem to manage to fall free onto the bottom of the aquarium, and even these manage to come through.

In actual breeding the parents will cooperate in the thorough cleaning job that most cichlids will go through prior to the deposition of their spawn. They seem to prefer a strip of slate about a foot long, three inches wide and ½-inch thick, slanted at a 30° angle to the glass of the aquarium, upon which to place their spawn. There seems to be no true correlation with spawning and the amount of light that is given, but angels do like some sunshine if possible. A resume of their likes and dislikes is as follows:

Light: part of the aquarium should, if possible, receive some direct rays of sunlight each day. Twelve hours of artificial light may be substituted for natural light. Though nothing definite is yet known, it is believed that the light cycle affects the spawning cycle.

Plants: heavily planted aquaria are necessary if the angelfish are maintained in a busy area. They

A *plecostomus*, or sucker-mouth catfish, *Pterygoplichthys gibbeceps. This fish should not be kept in the same aquarium as spawning angelfish, as it may eat the eggs!*

A new strain of angelfish has been developed and perfected in Singapore. The color of this fish turns from a normal gold and black to white. This spawning pair includes a white female which has already lost all her color and a male in the process of losing his color.

are "scary" fish and are frightened by shadows. They are best kept in aquaria heavily vegetated with Amazon sword plants or other stiff, broad-leafed plants. If maintained in an aquarium without plants, be sure that the tank is placed high enough to be out of sight of passers-by.

Temperature: between 68 and 90°F. Optimum breeding temperature is 80°F.

Water: must be clean and colorless. Slightly acid water from 6.6 pH to neutral (7.0) is best. Zero hardness.

THE FIREMOUTH CICHLID

The firemouth cichlid, *Cichlasoma meeki,* is not a fish to be kept with smaller fishes. It gets vicious and nasty and must never be kept with fishes smaller than itself. Why, then, are they kept at all? Because they are very colorful, they are interesting to breed, easy to breed and they show a maternal care for the eggs that defies description. When a pair are put together and they decide to spawn, the male, with his longer and more pointed anal and dorsal fins, will pick out a slate or piece of rock and clean it off. The female will then lay her eggs on this spot and the male will fertilize them. Then they take turns incubating the eggs by hovering over them and fanning them with their fins. Once the eggs have hatched, they will take care of the young and protect them against all harm. It is truly a sight to behold, so if you have a spare tank about, why not dedicate it to a pair of these cichlids?

OTHER NEW WORLD CICHLIDS

The angelfish and firemouth cichlid are just two of the many New World cichlids available to aquarium hobbyists. There are many others, variable in size and temperament and spawning behavior. On the small side of the scale are the "dwarf" cichlids such as the ram (*Microgeophagus ramirezi*) and various other species; on the larger side are the fishes of the genera *Aequidens* and *Cichlasoma*, as well as the popular oscar, *Astronotus ocellaris*. Cichlids in general are a very diverse group and are popular among fish hobbyists because of their interesting behavior as well as their good looks. Individual cichlid species, however, present difficulties in their maintenance because of their tendency toward aggressive behavior, and beginners in the hobby are advised to learn as much as they can about the individual species before making their selections. The books *Cichlids of the World* and *Dwarf Cichlids* provide comprehensive background information about these fishes.

MOUTH-BROODING CICHLIDS

As a whole, African mouth-brooding cichlids have had the most spectacular rise in popularity of any group of aquarium fishes. Their variety of brilliant colors, hardiness, ease of breeding and fascinating breeding behavior account for this mushrooming rise in popularity. The most popular types are the rock-dwellers or *mbuna*, as they are called by the native Malawians who collect them in Lake Malawi.

In these species, of which there are dozens, the eggs are laid on a rock and almost immediately picked up in the mouth by the female. The tissues of the lower part of the mouth stretch as more eggs are picked up. By the time spawning is complete, the female's mouth is literally bulging with eggs. She then swims off to a quiet place in the aquarium where she spends up to three weeks incubating the eggs and young in her mouth. During the incubation period the female usually does not eat at all. Finally, the mother ejects the young which are by now quite large and well able to fend for themselves. For a few days after the young are initially ejected, they seek shelter and protection from enemies in their mother's mouth. She willingly opens her mouth to let them in until they have grown too large to reenter. These colorful fishes seem to breed best in a community tank containing an assortment of mbuna species, but in order to save the mother from

A beautiful blueberry male zebra mbuna, Pseudotropheus zebra.

undue harassment during the incubation period and to prevent the babies from being eaten by the other fishes, the female should be moved to a tank of her own once the spawning is complete.

Some of the more popular mbuna are the zebra, *Pseudotropheus zebra*, which is available in an exciting array of color varieties, *Labeotropheus fuelleborni* and the rusty cichlid, *Iodotropheus sprengerae*...there are many more. There are a number of rock-dwelling cichlids from Lake Tanganyika, too. Some of them are mouth-brooders like the mbuna, but many of them are substrate brooders—they breed in a manner similar to that of the firemouth cichlids mentioned, except that they keep the eggs and young well concealed within the crevices of the rock clusters. So numerous are the species of rock-dwelling cichlids from these two lakes that several books have been written on these fishes alone. One of the most popular of these books, and certainly the most useful for helping readers to identify the various species from good color photos, is *African Cichlids of Lakes Malawi and*

Tanganyika, published by T.F.H. Publications.

ZEBRAFISH

Zebrafish, *Brachydanio rerio,* come from far-off India. They are very active fish, always on the move and extremely playful. They should be welcomed to every community aquarium, as they are peaceful and hardy in the bargain. Sex is extremely difficult to ascertain in this species and only the bloated appearance of the female is any sure sign of a sexual difference.

These fish lay non-adhesive eggs, and most professional breeders fill the bottom of their breeding tank with large marbles so their eggs can fall between the marbles and prevent the parents from gobbling them up as fast as they lay them.

The zebra will take all kinds of fish food, and will live to a ripe old age of 2½ years. Once they become hump-backed, it is a sign that they are getting on in years and should be disposed of. Usually, other fishes will kill the older members of the group.

A rusty cichlid, Iodotropheus sprengerae, *one of many species found in Lake Malawi.*

A mouth-brooder from Lake Malawi, Pseudotropheus microstoma, *having trouble getting all her young back into her mouth.*

These fish are best purchased in groups of four or six, as they tend to school and are a beautiful sight with their constant movement. The nickname zebra is a misnomer, as their stripes are not vertical as in the zebra, but are horizontal.

GIANT DANIO

The giant danio, *Danio malabaricus,* is a close relative to the zebrafish. This minnow comes from India and grows to a length of four inches. It is a fast-moving fish always on the go. It can jump quite a distance, so be sure that the aquarium is kept covered with a piece of glass.

They breed exactly as the zebras except that the eggs are adhesive, and they are as easily

A male Melanochromis johanni. *This species is found in Lake Malawi.*

fed. They require a temperature of 75°F, but can stand a variation of from 70 to 85°F without showing any ill effects. Smaller specimens should be purchased, as they are interesting to watch grow. This holds true for most fishes; buy them young, as not only are older fishes more expensive, but they will not live as long once you've purchased them (if a fish lives two years and he's 1½ years old when you buy him...well!).

PEARL DANIO

The pearl danio, *Brachydanio albolineatus*, is a fish closely related to both the giant danio and the zebrafish. It is smaller than the giant and gets a wee bit larger than the zebra. It, too, is a fast-swimming fish that takes on a shiny mother-of-pearl coloring flushed with red. If you look closely at it you will notice tiny barbels coming from its snout. This is characteristic, and the zebra has some, too.

Pearl danios will eat all types of food and require a temperature of 75°F, though they can stand a wide range up to 90°F. They are very difficult to sex and only a heavy female is a sure giveaway.

BARBS AND OTHER CYPRINIDS

All of the danios are members of the family *Cyprinidae*, a widely distributed family of fishes that includes a number of popular, colorful, inexpensive species besides the danios. It includes, for example, the group loosely referred to as the barbs, and it includes the very popular white cloud as well as a number of popular species known collectively (but very loosely) as "sharks."

Among the most popular of the barbs are the tiger barb (*Puntius tetrazona*), the cherry barb (*Puntius titteya*), the rosy barb (*Puntius conchonius*), the mirror barb (*Puntius oligolepis*) and Schwanenfeld's barb (*Puntius schwanenfeldi*). All of the species listed are from Asia; a few barb species also are occasionally imported from Africa, but they have never become very important in the aquarium hobby, even though some of them are good-looking fishes. Like the danios, the barbs are egg layers; they scatter eggs (varying in their degree of adhesiveness from species to species) among floating plants placed in bunches in the spawning tank.

The male drives the female back and forth through the tank until the female can be coaxed into proximity to a clump of plants and simultaneously into signaling to the male that she is ready to release her eggs, whereupon male and female embrace in a spawning contortion (usually accompanied by the male's bending himself around the female's body); the eggs are then expelled by the female in a shower. Spawning continues until the female is depleted of eggs. Spawning among the barbs often is a community affair, with many pairs taking part in the activities at the same time. Neither parent provides any care for the eggs. Both will eat them, in fact, and therefore should be removed from the spawning tank as soon after the spawning act as practicable. The eggs will hatch within a day or so if the tank is kept at a temperature of about 78°F; the fry are tiny (although not so tiny as the fry of anabantoid fishes like the betta and gouramis) and should be fed with the finest of live foods as soon as they have absorbed their yolk sacs and have become freeswimming. Fry of some barb species will be big enough to eat newly hatched brine shrimp immediately upon becoming freeswimming, but some require infusoria.

As a group the barbs are all fast-moving, active fishes continually on the prowl from one end of the tank to the other. They have high oxygen requirements

A giant danio, Danio malabaricus. *The giant danio is a cyprinid from India that is capable of growing to a length of four inches.*

Opposite, top left: A hatchetfish, Carnegiella strigata. *Opposite, top right:* A firemouth cichlid, Cichlasoma meeki, with its young. *Opposite, bottom:* A pair of blind cave characins. *Above:* The large fish are clown loaches and the smaller striped fish are tiger barbs; both are found in Asia. *Below:* South America's prize fish is the common brown discus, Symphysodon aequifasciata axelrodi.

and therefore should be kept in clean, well-aerated aquaria. They are fairly tolerant as far as temperatures are concerned, and some of them (the rosy barb is an example) will withstand water temperatures that are definitely non-tropical. Of the species listed here, Schwanenfeld's barb is by far the largest; fully mature individuals maintained in large aquaria will grow to over a foot in length. It usually is sold at only an inch or two in size, but purchasers should be aware of the fish's potential for growth. The tiger barb and cherry barb and mirror barb stay small (up to about two inches for the tiger barb, which is the largest of the three). The mirror barb and cherry barb are very peaceful, mind-their-own-business fishes, but the tiger barb has earned itself a reputation as a fin-nipper and perpetual haunter of slower-moving fishes. Tiger barbs are best maintained in groups of six or so if they are kept in a community aquarium with other fishes, because in that way they get a chance to work out their pestiness on each other and usually leave the other fishes alone.

The white cloud, *Tanichthys albonubes*, is another Asiatic cyprinid that has achieved great popularity in the tropical fish hobby. This undemanding species (which does better in cool water than in warm water) is probably the easiest of all egg-laying species to breed and raise. If kept in a tank by themselves, adult white clouds seem always to produce, without any effort on the part of the hobbyist, a number of fry that grow to a size at which they are recognizable as baby fish. Inexpensive and almost always available, the white cloud is a good all-around aquarium fish, especially for those who maintain small tanks, because this is a small species.

The family Cyprinidae also contains some other species that have attained great popularity. These are the *Labeo* species, the so-called "sharks," of which the red-tailed shark (*Labeo bicolor*) and the red-fin shark (*Labeo erythrurus*) are the most popular and most frequently offered for sale. Unlike the barbs and danios and white cloud, the *Labeo* species are not continuously active swimmers; they do things at a much less frantic pace and often take time out to rest in secluded hiding places in the tank. They like to glide leisurely around the aquarium, scraping algae from the aquarium glass and from plants and decorations in the tank. One problem with them, though, is that they often persecute other fishes, literally hounding them to death.

A red-tailed shark, Labeo bicolor, *a member of the family Cyprinidae.*

Left: *A male Siamese fighting fish,* Betta splendens, *tending its young.* **Below:** *A male Siamese fighting fish with bright coloration.*

Bubblenest Builders

SIAMESE FIGHTING FISH

The betta or Siamese fighting fish, *Betta splendens*, is undoubtedly the most beautiful fish that ever adorned an aquarium and is probably one of the most interesting. It has been bred in many different colors and, due to its popularity, will probably continue to be the subject of much experimental breeding.

The reproductive habits of the betta are most interesting. The male, as in most vertebrates, is the more gaily colored and the more notorious. He is distinguished from the female by having long, flowing, deeply colored fins that sometimes reach an inch or more in length. The female is seldom as colorful as the male and never has fins that can

be compared in size or beauty with those of the male.

As is true of most egg layers, bettas, both male and female, must be conditioned for their rites of reproduction. This conditioning process is a very old one used by many hobbyists with many types of birds, fishes and animals. It runs like this: the male and female are put in the same tank, being separated only by a glass partition (many aquarists make their own tanks of this type, but betta tanks are on the market just for this purpose). The male tries vigorously to reach the female, and the courting begins. The more frustrated he becomes the more deeply his colors show. Soon he realizes the uselessness of his efforts and starts to dance in front of the female, much like a male pigeon. This dance is really something to behold. With gills expanded and the look of a killer on his face, he suddenly dashes madly against the glass, trying vainly to get to the female. Fortunately, this mad capering subsides after a period of from four hours to several days, depending upon certain understandable factors, and then he starts to build a bubblenest. This bubblenest is a work of art. First the male betta gulps air from the surface of the water; this is easily done as the betta is one of a certain type of fish, called "labyrinth fish," that have an auxiliary set of "lungs" to help

their gills out. These "lungs" enable the bettas to live in a small receptacle, making excellent showpieces in a large goblet.

To get back to the bubblenest, we have observed the male betta take his gulp of air and now watch him "chew" on it for a second. Then he blows out a stream of bubbles. These bubbles undoubtedly can be compared to the mucous bubbles that we are capable of blowing. This process is repeated hundreds of times until a nest about 1½ inches in diameter is constructed. The nest may be high enough to be raised out of the water, sometimes reaching a thickness of about an inch. After the nest is complete, the glass partition must be removed very carefully (so as not to destroy the bubblenest), and the male and female are allowed to have their romance. This is by no means the end of the story. Let's look ahead.

When the partition has been removed you must be watching to make sure that the female is ready for the male. This is not easy to decide for the amateur, for it must be ascertained that the female has eggs to be fertilized. It will be noted that the female will seem a little heavier than before the seasoning process if she is ready. This is undoubtedly due to the many eggs that she is about to release.

When the male sees the female he will make a headlong dive for

Spawning among bettas begins with the male courting the female with spread fins and increased activity in building the bubblenest.

her, maybe ripping off a piece of her tail fin in his clumsy attempts. The female will probably hide in the foliage that must be provided at one end of the breeding tank just for this purpose. The rest of the tank must be free from any other material, including sand.

After a few hours of what looks like a fight to the finish, with the male chasing the female all around the tank, ripping off scales and tearing her fins to shreds, they will finally settle down to business. The male will wrap his body around the female and squeeze her until some eggs drop out, then he will quickly release the female and go down for the eggs and catch them in his mouth. These eggs are then blown into the bubblenest. This description obviously suggests why there must be no sand on the bottom of

Above: Blue gouramis of the marble strain. *Right:* Pearl gourami. *Below:* Zebra danio. *Opposite, top left:* Blue gourami, half-black strain. *Opposite, lower left:* Honey gourami. *Opposite, right:* A school of free-swimming fry eating microscopic infusoria. *Opposite, bottom:* Giant gourami.

this breeding tank. The eggs that the female drops are very small and are sand colored. If they should reach the bottom before the male has a chance to get them all up, then they will be lost and never develop into betta fry.

After the male has a mouthful of eggs and has blown them into his bubblenest, he then returns to his bride of the hour for more squeezing and consequently more eggs. This process may take hours but should never take more than a day at the most, since the fertilized eggs will start to hatch in two days. After the female has given up all her eggs, she must be removed or the male will surely kill her. The male should be left alone with the hatching fry for a few days to care for them.

The importance of the bubblenest can be seen easily, when it is realized that the young fry cannot withstand the great pressure at the bottom of the tank. The bubblenest keeps them at the surface, and they are thus able to be maintained at a minimum of water pressure. Should a fry get too active and burst its containing bubble, it will fall to the bottom where papa betta is waiting to catch it and blow it back to the top. This precaution may be necessary for as many as ten to 12 days, but care must be exercised that the male does not start to eat the young fry after that period of time. The best bet is to remove the male after ten days.

When the fry have hatched out, they must be fed a certain kind of live food that is called infusoria. An infusoria culture contains millions of microscopic animals that swim around in the water and can be compared with the daphnia or water fleas that we feed the larger variety of fish.

GOURAMIS

The betta might be the most popular of the species that are equipped with an auxiliary breathing apparatus and build a bubblenest, but it is far from the only one. A number of other species, some rivaling the betta in beauty of color and form, share the same peculiarities. Generally known as anabantoids, they make up a number of different families of fishes and many different genera. The most popular and commonly available of these fishes are called gouramis, and the most often seen aquarium gouramis are the blue gourami (*Trichogaster trichopterus*), the dwarf gourami (*Colisa lalia*), the pearl gourami (*Trichogaster leeri*) and the honey dwarf gourami (*Colisa chuna*).

The dwarf gourami is a peaceful and relatively small species. The male is an especially colorful fish, particularly at spawning time. The honey dwarf gourami, which has been an aquarium favorite for a much shorter time than the dwarf gourami, is less brilliantly colorful but equally pleasing. The pearl

A blue male gourami, Trichogaster trichopterus, *in breeding condition. Note the coloration on the edge of the anal fin.*

gourami is a much larger fish than either of the two *Colisa* species mentioned but is endowed with a sedate beauty all its own. It is an attractive fish even out of spawning time, but during spawning time the male adopts a wide area of bright orange, shading into red, over the belly and chest. The blue gourami, also called the three-spot gourami, is available in a number of different color patterns (opaline, golden, etc.). Roughly the same size as the pearl gourami, it is a much more combative species than the other three gourami species discussed thus far. This is not to say that it is a vicious fish—it's just that it is more aggressive than the other popular gouramis.

Because of their capacity to breathe atmospheric oxygen, the gouramis, like the betta, can withstand less-than-ideal tank conditions in the form of overcrowding, but again, like the betta, they are not to be kept under constantly poor conditions.

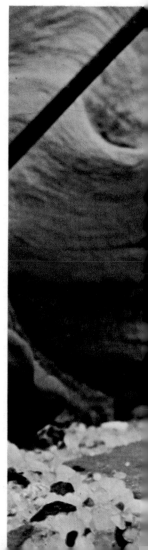

Above: The name "scavenger" is not really a proper designation for bottom-feeding fishes. The most desirable scavengers eat not only food that has fallen to the bottom of the tank but also algae from the glass and ornaments in the tank. A good example of such a scavenger is Gyrinocheilus aymonieri. *Right:* A spawning trio of Corydoras paleatus.

Scavengers

Among groups of living organisms, certain ones are destined to live upon the "leftovers." Fortunately for aquarium scavengers, most hobbyists tend to overfeed their fishes. This is one of the principal causes of death of fishes in captivity. DO NOT OVERFEED. Feed your fishes only as much as they can consume in ten minutes. For baby fishes this doesn't apply, as they must be fed as often as possible.

As the uneaten food particles

collect upon the bottom of the aquarium the water will start to become cloudy, the sand will turn black and the water will begin to give off an offensive odor. In order to allow a little more leeway as to overfeeding, certain types of catfishes are introduced into the aquarium to eat most of the uneaten food that has fallen to the bottom. Nearly all of these bottom-feeding catfishes belong to the genus *Corydoras*, and except for some color differences, they all have the same general body shape. Note that their mouths are positioned under the body and are flanked on each side by a barbel or whisker. They stick their snouts into the sand to dig out uneaten worms and other foods that have been ignored by the other fishes. The catfishes are nocturnal; they are active and eat at night, so don't think that the fish aren't doing their job. Have at least one catfish for every six other fishes in the aquarium.

A *"Chinese algae eater,"* Gyrinocheilus aymonieri. *This fish is an algae eater, although it is not Chinese.*

A pair of catfish, Corydoras trilineatus. *Note the typical barbels flanking their mouths.*

Not all fishes that are used as "scavengers" are catfishes. One very popular aquarium fish, well appreciated because of its habit of eating algal growths from the sides of the aquarium and from aquarium decorations, is *Gyrinocheilus aymonieri.* This fish is usually sold as a "Chinese algae eater," even though it doesn't come from China.

Snails are also scavengers, but they may eat the plants and do more harm than if they weren't used as scavengers. A few red ramshorn snails are all right, but keep away from any native snails.

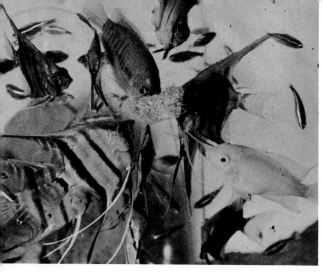

Freeze-dried foods were one of the author's first patented inventions. These photos were taken in the late 1950s, while these foods were being developed. **Above:** This photo shows the test to which the author put his freeze-dried tubifex worms to see if all the fishes enjoyed them. **Right:** Cardinal tetras attacking a piece of freeze-dried tubifex worms. The author raised these fish for 16 months on freeze-dried foods alone.

Fish Foods

Feeding your fish is very important. As has already been mentioned, DON'T OVERFEED YOUR FISHES. Fishes don't eat very much, so feed them sparingly, a little at a time.

FISH FOODS

Fish foods come under three categories: live foods, frozen foods, and prepared foods. The live foods are a necessary addition to your fishes' diet. Ask your shopkeeper for enough daphnia, tubifex or other live foods so that you may be able to feed your fishes enough for the one day. As a beginner it doesn't pay to try to raise your own live foods, but once you've gotten into the hobby in a real sort of way you'll want to look into these things.

Only buy enough live food to feed your fishes at a single serving. A small portion of worms or "bugs" (synonyms for tubifex and daphnia respectively) will be enough to feed 25 to 50 fishes a single meal. These live foods keep your fishes in good color and in good health.

Regular granulated and flake-form dried foods are good, as are freeze-dried foods.

It might help to offer your fish bits of scraped beef, in very fine pieces, or even bits of fish, clam

To keep your fish in good health and breeding condition, feed them a nutritious diet. Your pet shop owner can help you plan a well-balanced feeding regimen for your particular fishes.

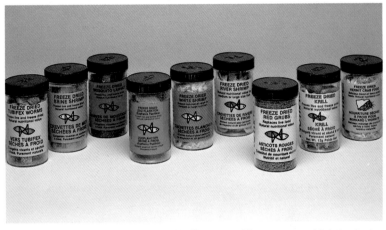

Above and below: Your pet shop will offer many different types of fish foods, including live, frozen, and prepared. In addition to these three types, there are different formulas for different fishes and for the different stages of the fishes' lives.

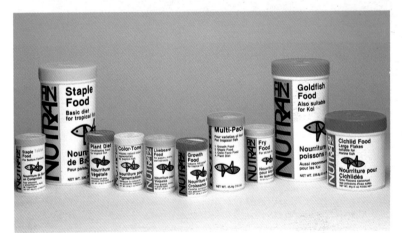

Above: Lake Malawi contains hundreds of very interesting cichlids. (Lake Malawi was once called Lake Nyasa, and this name is still used by the people of Tanzania). So does Lake Tanganyika! This pair of fish, Melanochromis auratus, *is from Lake Malawi.* **Opposite, top:** A magnificent split-tailed peach-colored betta has been developed from the wild fish. **Opposite, bottom:** The lyretail swordtail is a development from the 1960s. The future promises even more beautiful color varieties as the use of hormones, for interbreeding species and inducing spawning among hard-to-breed species, becomes more and more prevalent.

A trio of black tetras, Gymnocorymbus ternetzi. *This fish is rather aggressive but does well in a tank of larger fish.*

or crab. Shrimp is a delicacy, but be careful that only tiny bits are offered at a time, for these foods easily cloud the water.

Fresh frozen foods are excellent, especially brine shrimp; many different frozen foods are available.

Index

TROPICAL FISH
KW-020